Wonders of America

Yellowstone

For Brannon—M. D. B.

To Isaac's friend Tom—J. G. W.

ALADDIN PAPERBACKS
An imprint of Simon & Schuster Children's Publishing Division
1230 Avenue of the Americas, New York, NY 10020
Text copyright © 2008 by Marion Dane Bauer
Illustrations copyright © 2008 by John Wallace
READY-TO-READ, ALADDIN PAPERBACKS, and related logo
are registered trademarks of Simon & Schuster, Inc.
Designed by Christopher Grassi
The text of this book was set in Century Oldstyle.
Manufactured in the United States of America
First Aladdin Paperbacks edition April 2008
4 6 8 10 9 7 5
Library of Congress Cataloging-in-Publication Data
Bauer, Marion Dane.
Yellowstone / by Marion Dane Bauer ; illustrated by John Wallace.
p. cm.—(Wonders of America)
ISBN-13: 978-1-4169-5404-0 (pbk)
ISBN-10: 1-4169-5404-X (pbk)
ISBN-13: 978-1-4169-5405-7 (library)
ISBN-10: 1-4169-5405-8 (library)
1. Yellowstone National Park—Juvenile literature.
I. Wallace, John, 1966– II. Title.
F722.B395 2008
978.7'52—dc22
2007021618
0512 LAK

Wonders of America

Yellowstone

By **Marion Dane Bauer**

Illustrated by **John Wallace**

Ready-to-Read
ALADDIN
New York London Toronto Sydney

In 1872 the United States Congress set aside a large piece of land "for the benefit and enjoyment of the people."

FOR THE BENEFIT AND
ENJOYMENT OF THE PEOPLE

1872

1872

6

That place is
Yellowstone National Park.
It was the first national
park in the world.

Yellowstone is a magical place.
Superheated water shoots into
the air from geysers.

Springs and pools are
filled with hot water.

Steam rises from vents in the earth called fumaroles.

Mud holes bubble with gases.

One of the world's largest
petrified forests
is in Yellowstone.

Many animals make their
home there.

Bison and pronghorn antelope
live in Yellowstone.

Elk,

deer,

and bighorn sheep do too.

Visitors love seeing
black bears and grizzlies.

For many years no wolves
lived in Yellowstone.
People killed them off
to protect the deer and elk
that wolves hunt.

But we learned that
herds grow stronger
when wolves live near them.

Many people worked to bring wolves back to Yellowstone. Now the park has more than one hundred wolves.

Firefighters used to stop
all forest fires in Yellowstone.

27

But we learned that some
fires keep the forest healthy.

A national park
is a great place to
watch nature
at work.

Yellowstone National Park
still has a lot to teach us.

Interesting Facts about
Yellowstone National Park

★ Yellowstone began with an enormous volcanic eruption 2.1 million years ago. A second eruption occurred 1.3 million years ago. The most recent eruption was about 600 thousand years ago. Some day Yellowstone may erupt again.

★ There are about 1,000 geysers on our planet. Five hundred of them are in Yellowstone National Park.

★ Old Faithful is the most popular site in the park. It shoots water more than 100 feet into the air.

★ When the explorers Lewis and Clark went west, they didn't pass through Yellowstone. They heard about it from the Indians. One of Lewis and Clark's scouts, John Colter, went to explore. He is probably the first white man to see the wonders of Yellowstone.

★ Many people didn't believe the stories of Yellowstone when they first heard them. In 1871 the paintings of Thomas Moran and the photos of William Jackson proved to everyone that Yellowstone is real.

★ In 1988 a huge forest fire burned one third of the forests in Yellowstone. The fire also opened the cones of the lodgepole pine trees and dropped their seeds. Now the seeds are growing, and the forests are coming back.